Youthful Gray

Youthful Gray

The Poetry of Ray Rivera

RAY RIVERA

iUniverse, Inc.
Bloomington

Youthful Gray
The Poetry of Ray Rivera

iUniverse books may be ordered through booksellers or by contacting:

iUniverse
1663 Liberty Drive
Bloomington, IN 47403
www.iuniverse.com
1-800-Authors (1-800-288-4677)

ISBN: 978-1-4759-5613-9 (sc)
ISBN: 978-1-4759-5614-6 (ebk)

Library of Congress Control Number: 2012919319

Printed in the United States of America

iUniverse rev. date: 10/16/2012

Contents

This is to certify that

Ray Rivera

was elected into

The International Poetry Hall of Fame

In honor of this election, the

Ray Rivera Poetry Exhibit

has been established in The International Poetry Hall of Fame Museum.

This exhibit is located at

http://www.poets.com

on the Internet's World Wide Web.

Alex Hanley
Director

Introduction

My sister, Lita (one year my junior), and I were born in Harlem, New York. Our father, whom we never knew, abandoned us and our mother, Amparo Escalet. Because our mother was unable to care for us, we became wards of the state. The New York Foundling Hospital took in Lita and me when we were just one and two years old. We were then placed in a foster home for six years before ending up at an orphanage, the Little Flower Institute, for four more years. I was bedridden for most of that time with rheumatic fever.

Lita and I were finally released back into the custody of our mother when we were eleven and twelve years old. Sadly, our mother was living with a man who would go on to abuse us all. After horrendous treatment that included a severe beating with a metal pipe that almost cost me my eye, I stood up to this man. He then threw me out of the house. While on the streets and weak from hunger, I wandered into an eatery on 103rd Street, Paul's Restaurant, and asked the owner if I could work for my food. He agreed, and I peeled potatoes in the basement during the evening for five dollars a week plus meals. During the mild months, I slept on rooftops and in parks. When winter came, I slept in hallways with a hot container of coffee from Paul's to keep me warm. Soon, however, my health started to fail. I was too frightened to tell anyone, fearing a return to the orphanage. Eventually, I went to Mt. Sinai Hospital with terrible chest pain, high fever, and malnutrition. I had pneumonia, and my condition was critical. I remained in Mt. Sinai Hospital for half a year.

During this time, I met a professor of philosophy who happened to be convalescing in the bed next to me. With very little education, I could barely read, and I had a very limited vocabulary. The man helped me learn how to read. He then gave me a book, which set in motion ideas about nature in my mind. I was soon transferred to Montefiore Hospital for further treatment. As I began to feel better, the nurses would wheel me onto the hospital grounds where I could see and hear the sounds of nature.

What I experienced inspired me to write many of the following poems. Poetry, and later music, helped heal my wounds.

Bluebird Serenade

I never knew what nature was like
Until my bluebird came in sight.
I met him early one summer morn
Upon the tree in my little lawn.

He was singing in a lovely way,
Telling me of the month of May.

He wakes me up in the early dawn
To serenade my every morn.

The singing is beautiful;
The world is so gay
When they hear the bluebird serenade.

Nature's Symphony

Nature's own symphony is beautiful and gay;
She put it in this world, and it's here to stay.
I listen to it every day when I'm out alone,
Out in the woods where I love to roam,
Where there's plenty of animals to make music all day
In their own happy little way.

Birds sit on the treetops and sing all day,
Sing about nature,
Sing of the day in many strange ways,
While crickets keep calling from out in the swamps.
Sing on, you birds, make the music more gay.

This is nature out in the woods,
Meaning birds, flowers, trees, and every other thing
Which brings up nature's symphony.

Glorious Morning

The sun is just about to come up;
The clock has started ringing.
A voice is saying with a sweet tone of music,
"Come out and seek me;
I'm the glorious morning."

The hills look so beautiful,
People so gay.
Everyone seems to be on his way
On to the farmlands, ready to work,
And thank the Lord for a glorious morning.

I'm Happy

Woke up this morning 'bout a quarter to nine,
Looked out the window, started feelin' fine.
The sun was out;
The sky was clear.
No more pollution, brother, anywhere.

Now I'm happy;
Yeah, I'm happy.
I'm so happy;
I've got happiness all over me.

The world had a meeting just the other day;
They all got up, and they all had a say.
Now you dig,
And I'll dig you.
Let's get together;
It's the thing to do.

There'll be no more talking 'bout droppin' the bomb.

Why should we do anyone some harm

When things get rough?

We'll sit and talk;

We'll all join hands and then just take a walk.

So Still Is the Night

So still is the night
When you're not around.
So still is the night
Without a love song.
I'm wearing a frown;
Love's upside down
So still is the night.

Since you are gone
The music has stopped.
So still is my heart
That once beat in tune.
So still is the night,
So still is the night.

Setting a Dream

I'm setting a dream to music,
A dream that may one day come true,
By writing a symphony of nature
And the things it does for you.

It makes your eyes so bright at night
When stars are up above,
And you make it more beautiful,
My one and only love.

When I am out alone at night
I hear my symphony,
A symphony I'm setting to a dream,
Which I know is you.

The running water in the brook,

The howling of the wind,

The waves that rush upon the beach

Come so far in that they're within our reach.

I see you on the seashore

When the sun is going down;

You help to make the sun more bright,

Then help create my symphony.

Wake Up

Wake up, you sleepers;
Wake up and hear
The bells that are ringing
That springtime is here.

Look out the window;
Look out the earth.
See all the farmers plowing the dirt.

The air is so wonderful;
People look gay.
Children are singing;
It's springtime in May.

We Sing

We sing of the ocean.
We sing of the sea,
Sing about nature,
And of the wonderful trees,
Of the rainstorms,
And the rain
As it falls on lovers' lane.

All lovers are waiting,
Ready to start to sing
Of the rainstorms.

As soon as it passes,
The birds started singing
Before we could start.
Their music is beautiful,
And so is each heart.

The world hears the music.

Each heart is aflame with love.

I am sure that will always remain.

Each heart is together;

None is apart,

To the tune of such music

Deep down in their hearts.

March 20, 1991.

Mr. Ray Rivera
3235 Emmons Avenue
Brooklyn, New York 11235

Dear Ray:

Congratulations for being chosen Golden Poet of 1991. Your poem "Free America" expresses the feelings of many, and most Americans in the face of an most recent are in Saudi Arabia. Expressions which has been reflected in the news media and TV of America's feelings, seem well by your poem. I congratulate you for continuing to be one of America's leading composer and song writer. Best wishes to your family.

Sincerely,

Sherman E. Dix, ACSW

SED/eo

Wrapped Up in the Blues

Yesterday I was wrapped up in happiness.
Today I'm wrapped up in the blues,
All because I believed you'd love me,
Love me till the end of time.

But when I awoke this morning, I found you gone.
You left a note telling me,
Yes, telling me,
That you found yourself a new love.

And so I'm wrapped up in the blues,
Wrapped up so tight,
Think I will die.
All I can do is cry, cry, cry
'Cause I'm so wrapped up in the blues.

Hobo World

Hobo life they say is bad;
Some even say it's mighty sad.
Sad to you but not to me
'Cause I have much fun and travel free.

A bed for a quarter,
A shave for a dime.
The beds have roaches,
And still it's fine.

A bottle of beer,
A bottle of rum
Is what I need to keep on the run.

Don't you people envy me
When you see I have such liberty.

Jazz

Jazz! Blue Monk played by Thelonious Monk Jazz! Lady Day singin' 'bout her "lover man" Jazz! Stan Getz and the girl from Ipanema. Hey, dig Jackie Williams, Mr. Cool himself beatin' time on "Caravan" Jazz! Hank Jones, piano playin' is such a delight. Have you heard Horace Silver play "Song For My Father" or Billy Taylor play "Ray's Tune" as only he can Jazz! Lester Young leaps in with his cool, cool sound Jazz! Ella sings 'bout the moon, while Dakota Station tells you of the late, late show Jazz! Count Basie is down for the count 'cause Joe Williams has the blues Jazz! I've got a hunch that's John Bunch on that Edgar Sampson tune Jazz! Have you taken a trip on Route 66 with Nat King Cole 'cause, if you haven't, Duke Ellington will take you for a ride on the A-Train Jazz! Major Holly, Slam Stewart, Milt Hinton, Richard Davis, Ray Brown, Red Mitchell, can you picture them all playin' together Jazz! Feet tappin' to the drumbeat of Papa

Jo Jones, Ray Mosca, Cozy Cole, Percy Brice, Art Blakely, Buddy Rich, Louie Belson, and Max Roach. The beat goes on and on Jazz! The guitar of Gene Bertoncini on a soulful bossa nova. Kenny Burrell playin' the Blues. Wes doin' it his way. The rhythm of Freddy Green Jazz! Paul Desmond takin' five while Yard Bird Charlie Parker let's you know that now's the time for Jazz! So many past and present have given to this great American art form we call Jazz!

Improvise

Improvise your day with a song;
Improvise as you go along.
Give out with some laughter
And you will find thereafter
Your day filling up with happiness.

Health Is Wealth

Health is wealth,
That's for sure.
Without your health,
Money and riches don't mean a thing.

So take good care of yourself,
Lay off the smoking and drugs,
Think positive as you start your day,
And you'll feel better in every way.

The Mind

The mind is a powerful tool;
Don't let it go to waste.
Let it work the way it should.

Here's to Storme Williams

Here's to Storme Williams,
A great country singer of songs,
With a voice like the gentle sound
Of a cool evening spring rain
Raining down music and love songs.

Here's to Storme Williams,
A great country singer of songs,
Out in front of a crowd
From one to a thousand.
His voice comes in strong,
Singing songs you want to hear.

Hear people cheer,
And they yell out loud,
"Hey, Storme, give us another song."

Oh, man, you can't go wrong
With a voice like yours;
You can conquer the world
Of country music again and again.
So let's hear it
One more time.

Here's to Storme Williams,
That great country singer,
That singer of country songs.

Save the Earth

Let's get together and save the earth
By getting rid of all this dirt.
Let's recycle all our waste
So we can have a cleaner place.
Stop throwing garbage on the ground
'Cause it will pile up by the pound.

We have to find a good solution
To rid the world of its pollution.
Fish are dying in the sea.

I can't believe what I see:
People getting cancer, it's all around,
Toxins seeping up from the ground.

Think of the children, yours and mine;
What will they find in years to come?

We have to find a good solution
To rid the world of its pollution.

Here's to the Girl

Here's to the girl
Who gives me happiness.

Here's to the girl
Who gives me love.

Here's to the girl
Who gives me peace of mind
As I go on through life.

Here's to the girl
Who gives me laughter.

Here's to the girl
Who makes me smile.

Here's to the girl
Who says she'll always care
And whose love I share.

Here's to the girl
Who is from that Isle of Staten.

Here's to the girl
Who holds my hand.

Here's to the girl
Who says she loves me.

To her and only her
I wish both happiness and love.

We Are Your Children

We are your children, so give us a chance.
Stop the wars, the violence, and the drugs.
We are your children, so give us a chance.
Our lives have just begun.

Stop the pollution, hatred, and fighting.
We learn from you, our elders.
We depend on you, our elders.
If you can't get it together,
What chance do we have?

Hey, we are your children, so give us a chance.
All we're asking is a chance at life.
Stop the abuse of the young ones.
Stop doing crack.
Stop the killings.

We are your children, so give us a chance.

For, without that chance,

What have we to look forward to?

Yes, we are your children, so give us a chance.

You Will Walk That Road

I saw an elder couple pass me by,
And as I thought about it,
I said to myself,
You will walk that road one day,
So think about giving up that seat
On a bus or train.

Or be kind and lend a hand
'Cause there's no escaping it.
You will walk that road one day;
You won't stay young forever.

Sadness of a Father

Feeling sad about the aloofness of a son

Whose father loves him very much,

So sad toward the aloofness

Of his daughters who never call

Just to say hello and say,

"How are you, Dad?"

Where is that love we once shared?

As father to son, as father to daughters,

Could their growing up have changed them that much

As to not even send a card

Of wishes at holiday time?

Oh, the hidden tears of a sad, sad dad
Who wonders about a time that used to be,
Sharing and caring
About children he loved and still does.

The hidden hurt within,
The feeling of emptiness.
Will he leave this world
Without those last wonderful words of
"We love you, Dad"?

Ted Turner Blues

I heard Ted Turner speaking on TV;
The things he was saying
Just hit home with me.
The way that things can happen,
One can never tell.
It happened to Ted Turner;
I'm glad it wasn't me.

You can lose seven billion dollars
And lose everything you own,
But crying over spilled milk
Will only bring you down.

So get your life together
Is what Ted Turner said,
'Cause crying over spilled milk
Won't get you anywhere.

What's done is done,
So look ahead.
Forget the past,
Just like Ted Turner said.

You can't cry over spilled milk
Or sit around and mope
Are the things Ted Turner said
When I heard him on TV.

Youthful Gray

Even though my hair is gray
I'm full of life in every way.
I never say, "I wish I were young"
'Cause I'm youthful gray in every way.

Negativity is not part of me;
I do positive affirmations every day.

My health is good;
My mind is clear.
My youthfulness gives me the will
To erase all stress from within
And keep my mind on a healthful trip.

I never feel that I'm getting old;
I'm only getting mellow,
Like vintage wine
Whose taste gets better with time.

So when your hair starts turning gray,
Don't think of it as getting old;
Just think of it as youthful gray.

Crystal

10/02

Dear Ray,

Thank you for letting me read your poem. It really hits home. It is very special.

Hope you are doing well.

Wish you the best

Crystal Hyde

Obama and Michelle

When Obama met Michelle
He was happy as could be,
Took one look at her,
Said, "She's the one for me."
Michelle, you're the one for me.

I love the way you walk.
I love the way you talk.
I love the way you smile.
When I look into your eyes,
Michelle, you're the one for me.

Oh, yeah,
There's no one but you.
No one but you.
No one but you, Michelle.

Kenny and Michelle

When Kenny met Michelle
He was happy as could be,
Took one look at her,
Said, "She's the one for me."
Michelle, you're the one for me.

I love the way you walk.
I love the way you talk.
I love the way you smile.
When I look into your eyes,
Michelle, you're the one for me.

Oh, yeah,
There's no one but you.
No one but you.
No one but you, Michelle.

The Library

I've traveled the world
through books I've read
at the public library.

I learned of continents and their cultures,
of people I've never met,
by reading books at the public library.

Read about philosophies, art, music,
and of medical wonders
by reading books at the public library.

There is so much to learn
and the learning is free,
so take a tip from me
and read a book at the public library.

CHARLES B. RANGEL
15TH CONGRESSIONAL DISTRICT
NEW YORK

COMMITTEE:
WAYS AND MEANS
RANKING MEMBER

JOINT COMMITTEE ON TAXATION

☐ 2354 RAYBURN HOUSE OFFICE BUILDING
WASHINGTON, DC 20515-3215
TELEPHONE: (202) 275-4365

DISTRICT OFFICE:
MS. VIVIAN E. JONES
DISTRICT ADMINISTRATOR

☐ 163 WEST 125TH STREET
NEW YORK, NY 10027
TELEPHONE: (212) 663-3900

PLEASE RESPOND TO
OFFICE CHECKED

Congress of the United States
House of Representatives
Washington, DC 20515-3215

January 17, 2006

Ray Rivera
3235 Emmons Avenue, Suite #718
Brooklyn, New York 11235

Dear Mr. Rivera:

Thank you for the wonderful packet you prepared detailing some of your work and accolades. You are truly gifted and your work will forever be a testament to the power of your pen and the depth of your prose. I was stuck by the subtly with which you underscore the power of reading in "The Library." I am happy that the national Library of Poetry published this piece in The Rippling Waters.

I wish you the best of luck in the coming years. May your ink pen never dry and your imagination continue to run wild!

Sincerely,

Charles B. Rangel
Member of Congress

CBR/djj

July 11, 2002

Ms. Siobhan Reardon
Acting Executive Director
Office of the Executive Director
Brooklyn Public Library
Central Library
Grand Army Plaza
Brooklyn, New York 11238

Dear Ms. Reardon:

  I am writing concerning a request from Mr. Ray Rivera, 3235 Emmons Avenue, Suite 718, Brooklyn, New York 11235, that the Brooklyn Public Library consider using his poem entitled "Library" as the official poem of the library. Recently, I had the privilege of meeting Mr. Rivera, an accomplished jazz musician, who performed at the 25th anniversary celebration of Brooklyn's community boards on June 24, 2002 at Brooklyn Borough Hall. As clearly indicated by the enclosed documents, Mr. Rivera is not only a well-respected jazz musician, but a very talented poet as well.

  I hope you share my enthusiasm for Mr. Rivera's poetry and consider using the "Library" as the official poem of the Brooklyn Public Library.

  Thank you for your kind consideration.

Sincerely,

Marty Markowitz

Enclosures

Cc: Ray Rivera

MM/ef

The American Legion

American Legion, four brave chaplains who gave up their life jackets and lives on the USAT *Dorchester* so other men could be saved. American Legion, legionnaires on the march for peace. Men and women of all faiths and religions fighting side by side on foreign shores to help keep the American dream alive. American Legion, bravery in the face of great opposition and danger. American Legion, the best of Americanism, taking a stand to keep the American flag flying high and proud for God and country. American Legion, remembering those who gave their lives in a time of great sacrifice so we, our families, and children could go on living the American dream. American Legion, knowing the meaning of flag, faith in our country, loyalty to our country, armor for our country, and glory of our country. Remembering the men and women who fought and those who gave their lives to keep the red, white, and blue. Proud to wave our flag so all can see and know the meaning of the American way. American Legion, Americanism at its best. The land of the free, land of the brave, and freedom for everyone regardless of race, color, and creed. American Legion, standing up for what we believe in, standing up for all to share Americanism in this great country of ours.

Free America

The singing and laughter, the playing of children
Is what we all want in a country that's free.
We don't want war, but we all want peace
To help keep our country as free as can be.

Free country, free land
Means America to all,
The home of the brave and the free.

So let's keep America the way it is
And live like a Yank should live.
Then for centuries and centuries, we can all say,
"America, America is the place for me."

Printed in the United States
By Bookmasters